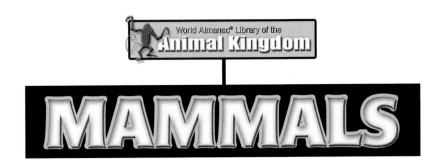

MAMMALS

Sarah Wilkes

WORLD ALMANAC® LIBRARY

Please visit our web site at: www.worldalmanaclibrary.com
For a free color catalog describing World Almanac® Library's list of high-quality books
and multimedia programs, call 1-800-848-2928 (USA) or 1-800-387-3178 (Canada).
World Almanac® Library's fax: (414) 332-3567.

Library of Congress Cataloging-in-Publication Data

Wilkes, Sarah, 1964-
    Mammals / by Sarah Wilkes.
        p. cm. — (World Almanac Library of the animal kingdom)
    Includes bibliographical references and index.
    ISBN 0-8368-6212-0 (lib. bdg.)
    1. Mammals—Juvenile literature. I. Title.
    QL706.2.W585   2006
    599—dc22   2005052627

This North American edition first published in 2006 by
World Almanac® Library
A Member of the WRC Media Family of Companies
330 West Olive Street, Suite 100
Milwaukee, WI 53212 USA

Subject Consultant: Jane Mainwaring, Natural History Museum
Editor: Polly Goodman
Designer: Tim Mayer
Illustrator: Jackie Harland
Picture research: Morgan Interactive Ltd and Victoria Coombs
World Almanac® Library art direction: Tammy West
World Almanac® Library editor: Carol Ryback
World Almanac® Library cover design: Jenni Gaylord

Photo credits: (t) top; b (bottom); l (left); right (r).
Cover photograph: the face of a cheetah.
Title page (clockwise from tl): noctule bat, European mole, West Indian manatee, lion.
Chapter collage (top to bottom): macro photographs of the fur or skin of a giraffe, leopard,
elephant, zebra, and brown bear.
CORBIS: Images.com cover. Ecoscene: / Hugh Clark title page (tl), 17; / Steve Austin title
page (tr), 11; / Fritz Pölking title page (bl), 5, 19(t), 32, 33, 34, 36, 38, 40; / Phillip Colla
title page (br), 28, 29, 30, 31; / Owen Newman 4; / Michael Maconachie 8; / Wayne Lawler
9; / Robin Redfern 10, 25, 26; / Judyth Platt 12; / Robert Pickett 13, 18, 19(b), 20, 43;
/ Michael Gore 21; / Peter Cairns 24, 39; / Luc Hosten 37; / Karl Ammann 42.
naturepl.com: / Dave Watts 6; / Pete Oxford 7; / Dietmar Nill 14, 16; / John Downer 22;
/ Mark Brownlow 23; / John Cancalosi 27; / Eric Baccega 35; / Anup Shah 41.

Printed in China

1 2 3 4 5 6 7 8 9 10 09 08 07 06

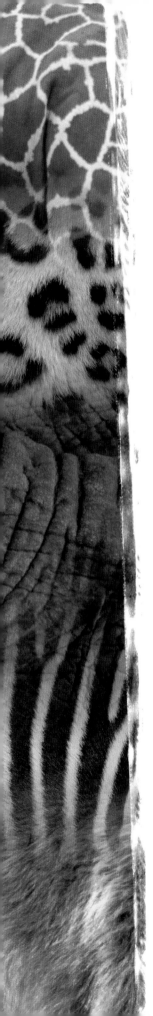

CONTENTS

It is not possible to include information about every mammal species in this book.
A taxonomic chart for mammals appears on page 44.

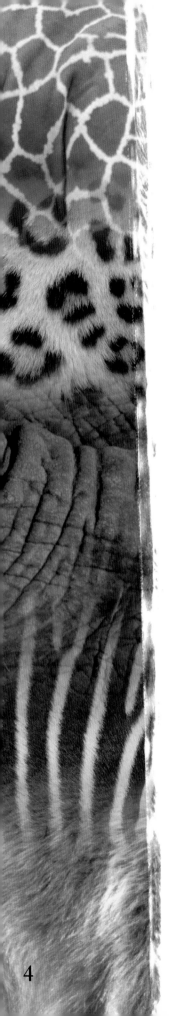

WHAT ARE MAMMALS?

Mammals are among the best-known animals in the world. They range from the gigantic blue whale to the tiny pygmy shrew, from whales and dolphins to hedgehogs and humans.

Mammal features

Mammals are a class of vertebrates to which humans belong. They are part of the phylum Chordata. All vertebrates have a vertebral column—a series of small bones that runs down their back. There are about forty-six hundred species of mammals, and new species are still being discovered.

Kangaroos are marsupials. This red kangaroo (*Macropus rufus*) carries a joey (young kangaroo).

Mammals have many characteristics in common. The name *mammal* comes from the mammary glands from which female mammals produce milk for their young. Most mammals are covered in hair. Mammals have four types of teeth—incisors, canines, premolars, and molars—that are adapted to suit their diet. Internally, all mammals have a sheet of muscle, called the diaphragm, that divides the chest from the abdomen. Mammals are endothermic, or warm-blooded. Their body temperature stays within a very narrow range regardless of the outside temperature. For example, the human body temperature is approximately 98.6 °Fahrenheit (37 °Celsius).

Subclasses

Mammals are divided into three subclasses: monotremes, marsupials, and placental mammals. Monotremes lay eggs, while marsupials give birth to tiny, immature young that live in their mother's pouch, feeding on her milk until they are well grown. Placental mammals give birth to well-developed young, some of which can run around within minutes of birth.

CLASSIFICATION

Biologists have identified several million unique organisms. They group together those with shared characteristics. The classification system moves through general to specific categories until each organism receives an exact binomial classification: a "last" name—the genus—and a "first" name—the species. The animal kingdom is divided into phyla (singular: phylum). Each phylum is divided into classes (also super- and subclasses), which are divided into orders (also super- and suborders) and then into families, genera (singular: genus), and species. A genus and species names a single organism that differs from all other organisms. In most cases, only members of the same species can reproduce with each other to produce fertile offspring.

The classification of the African elephant (*Loxodonta africana*) is shown on the right.

KINGDOM: Animal

PHYLUM: Chordata

CLASS: Mammalia

ORDER: Proboscidea

FAMILY: Elephantidae

GENUS: *Loxodonta*

SPECIES: *africana* (African elephant)

Use the first letter of each word in this sentence to remember the classification order:
Kings **P**lay **C**hess **O**n **F**ridays, **G**enerally **S**peaking.

The subclasses are divided into twenty-six smaller groups called orders. Mammals in the same order have certain unique features in common.

This books looks at the orders of mammals, their characteristics, and the way each group of mammals has adapted to its environment.

The African elephant (*Loxodonta africana*) is a placental mammal and the largest land mammal. Young elephants, called calves, feed on milk for up to three years.

EGG LAYERS (MONOTREMATA)

When biologists first studied the duck-billed platypus in 1798, they found it had the beak and webbed feet of a duck and a flat, beaver-like tail. It was like no other animal, so they placed it in an order of its own: Monotremata.

The duck-billed platypus (*Ornithorhynchus anatinus*) uses its webbed feet to propel itself through the water.

Laying eggs

Mammals in the order Monotremata are known as monotremes. They are unusual mammals that lay eggs. There are only three species of monotremes: the duck-billed platypus and two species of echidna, or spiny anteater. Monotremes are found only in Australia (including Tasmania) and on the island of New Guinea.

Monotremes have a long snout or bill and, as adults, they have no teeth. The word *monotreme* means "one hole," which refers to their one lower opening, the cloaca. The gut, reproductive, and urinary systems all open into the cloaca.

Duck-billed platypus

The platypus is a semi-aquatic animal that lives in streams and rivers. It has a streamlined body and webbed feet. The platypus finds food using its sensitive bill rather than sight. Thick fur insulates its body against cold water temperatures. Winter temperatures in Australia and Tasmania and the mountaintops of New Guinea can fall below freezing.

The female platypus lays one or two soft-shelled eggs in a nest at the end of an underground burrow. She incubates them (keeps them warm) for ten days until they hatch. The young platypuses feed on milk that oozes out through her fur.

Echidnas

Echidnas are covered in long spines that are used for defense. If threatened by predators, echidnas curl up into a ball, just like porcupines. They have small, beady eyes and a long, narrow snout. Short-beaked echidnas use their long, sticky tongue to lick up ants and termites. Echidnas locate their prey in the undergrowth using their sense of smell instead of their eyesight. After a short-beaked echidna locates a nest of ants or termites, it rips open the nest with its powerful claws. The long-beaked echidna uses its spiny tongue to hook earthworms.

Short-beaked echidnas are usually diurnal (active during the day), usually during the cooler times near dawn and dusk. During the hot summer months, they often become nocturnal (active at night). They escape the heat of the day by burying themselves in soft soil.

The echidna (*Tachyglossus aculeatus*) uses its long snout and excellent sense of smell to find its insect prey.

POUCHED MAMMALS (MARSUPIALS)

Marsupials are pouched mammals. Kangaroos, wombats, koalas, and possums are considered Australian marsupials and live in Australia, Tasmania, and the surrounding islands. Different varieties of opossums are found throughout North and South America. Marsupials live in a wide variety of habitats, including grasslands, forests, and cities. Most display nocturnal tendencies.

The female koala (*Phascolarctos cinereus*) gives birth to a single offspring, called a joey. When it is six months old, the joey leaves the pouch and is carried on its mother's back.

Caring for their young

Marsupials are an unusual subclass of mammals. They differ from placental mammals because they give birth to their young after a very short pregnancy. The newborn young are poorly developed and completely dependent on their mother. Most female marsupials have a pouch. Immediately after birth, the tiny babies crawl up their mother's fur into her pouch, where they attach themselves to a teat (nipple). They feed on their mother's milk until they are large enough to leave the safety of the pouch. The North American Virginia opossums have huge litters, sometimes in excess of twenty young, but they do not all survive—the female has only thirteen teats. The young ride on their mother's back when they no longer fit in her pouch.

Getting around

Marsupials use many different methods to move around, depending on their habitat. Kangaroos and wallabies live on open grasslands and use koalas, and tree kangaroos live in woodlands and have long claws to grip and climb trees. The sugar or honey glider possom uses folds of skin from the back of the forelimb to the front of the hindlimb to glide through the air from tree to tree. Wombats and marsupial moles are burrowing marsupials. Their muscular shoulders and thick neck are ideal for digging. Many Western Hemisphere opossums have adapted to living in urbanized areas.

Marsupial food

Most marsupials are omnivores that feed on a mixed diet of plant and animal foods. Some, like the koala, are herbivorous. Carnivorous marsupials include the quolls, kowaris, and Tasmanian devils. The Tasmanian devil is a fierce hunter that preys on insects, small birds, and other marsupials.

The brush-tailed possum (*Trichosurus vulpecula*) is a common sight in Australian backyards at night. It uses its prehensile tail to help it climb.

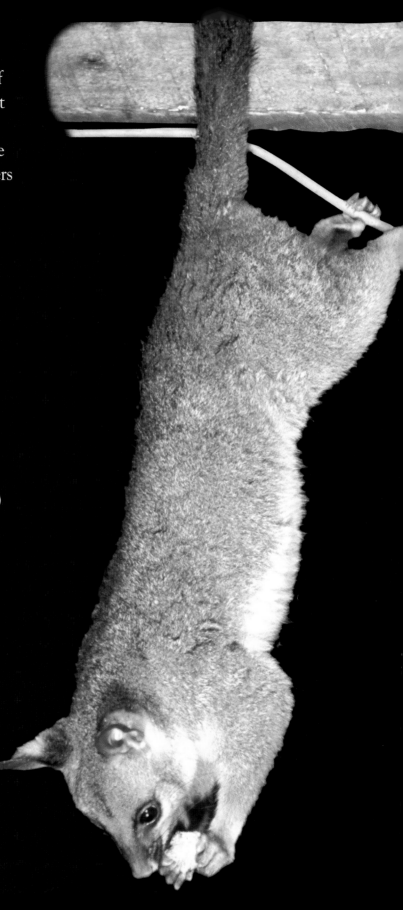

KEY CHARACTERISTICS
MARSUPIALS

- **Young born at an early stage of development.**
- **Presence of a pouch in which young are suckled.**
- **First toe of hind foot is either absent or lacks a claw.**
- **Body temperature is lower than that of placental mammals.**
- **Most marsupials have more teeth than placental mammals.**

INSECT EATERS (INSECTIVORA)

Insectivores are small, busy mammals that live all over the world, except for the polar regions and Australia. They range in size from the tiny pygmy white-toothed shrew, which is just 2 inches (5 centimeters) long and weighs about 0.07 ounces (2 grams), to the moonrat, which can grow up to 18 inches (46 cm) long and can weigh as much as 4 pounds (2 kilograms).

Sensitive whiskers on the nose, tail, and other parts of its body help the mole (*Talpa europaea*) find its favorite prey—worms.

Insectivores form the third-largest order of mammals after bats and rodents, with about 370 species. The order includes well-known animals, such as shrews, moles, and hedgehogs, as well as the lesser-known solenodons, desmans, and tenrecs.

Twitchy noses

Most insectivores are nocturnal and sleep during the day. Shrews are different from most insectivores because they are diurnal. Insectivores are usually solitary creatures. An insectivore has a pointed head with tiny eyes and ears. Vision is not particularly important to insectivores because they are nocturnal. They rely on their other senses to find food. The part of the brain that is responsible for an insectivore's sense of smell is remarkably large. This gives them an excellent sense of smell that they use along with touch to find prey, such as small insects, worms, and slugs.

One of the most noticeable features of an insectivore is its long, twitchy snout surrounded by sensitive whiskers. The solenodon has a particularly long snout to forage for food in the undergrowth. The star-nosed mole has a strange-looking nose that ends in a mass of pink tentacles that are extremely sensitive to touch.

Not just insects

The teeth of insectivores are pointed and suited to crushing the bodies of insects. Although the name *insectivore* suggests that they eat just insects, they eat a range of other prey too, including worms, snails, slugs, and birds' eggs. Water shrews may catch small fish and frogs.

Moving around

Insectivores have four short legs and five clawed toes on their feet. Insectivores are flat-footed, which means they walk with the soles and heels of their feet on the ground. They can walk, run, and climb, but they cannot leap. The rare web-footed tenrec has sharp claws that help it swim and grip slippery rocks.

The common shrew (*Sorex araneus*) has a pointed head with a long snout and tiny eyes. The ears are small and not visible through its fur.

Adaptation to habitat

Insectivores are specially adapted to their habitats in different ways. The mole, for example, is adapted to living underground. Its body is streamlined for digging, and it has huge front paws with long claws ideally suited to digging out tunnels. Its short, thick fur can lie at any angle, allowing the animal to move forward or backward in a tight tunnel. The mole is virtually blind. Instead of using sight, it uses its whiskers and sense of smell to locate worms and other animals that fall into the tunnels.

Hedgehogs (*Erinaceus europeaus*) use their long spines for defense. When under attack, they curl up into a tight ball so that their spines are sticking out.

Surviving winter

Hedgehogs cannot find enough food in winter to survive, so they go into a deep sleep called hibernation. During the autumn months, they build up their fat reserves by eating lots of food. Then they make a nest for themselves under a pile of leaves and hibernate. During hibernation, hedgehogs' body temperature falls from about 100 °F (38 °C) to just 39 °F (4 °C), which means they do not use much energy to keep warm. Their heartbeat slows, and they breathe only a few times every minute. When the temperature rises in the spring, their body temperature rises and they wake up.

Poisonous bite

The North American short-tailed shrew, the European water shrew, and the solenodon defend themselves with a poisonous bite that stuns their prey. These insectivores and the male playtpus are the only poisonous mammals. Solenodons are very rare. They are found only on two islands in the Caribbean—Cuba and Hispaniola. Their numbers have been decreasing because their forest habitat is being destroyed for farmland. They also have been killed by animals, such as dogs, cats, rats, and mongooses, that are not native to the islands.

Extra orders: tree shrews, elephant shrews, and colugos

Tree shrews, elephant shrews, and colugos (flying lemurs), were once considered insectivores. Each is now reclassified into a separate order. Tree shrews are small, squirrel-like mammals with well-developed senses. They feed on small animals, such as insects. Elephant shrews, as their name suggests, have a long and very sensitive snout. They can run quickly on their powerful back legs. Colugos glide through the air between trees using a winglike flap of skin that stretches between their limbs.

Tree shrews (*Tupaia* sp.) are small, secretive mammals. Food passes quickly through their simple gut, so they must eat for much of the day to survive.

KEY CHARACTERISTICS
INSECTIVORA

- **Long snout with wet nose and whiskers.**
- **Presence of a cloaca.**
- **Five toes on each foot.**
- **Flat-footed.**
- **Relatively small brain.**

BATS (CHIROPTERA)

Bats, such as this noctule bat (*Nytalus noctula*), move their wings up and down, just like a bird in flight.

Bats are the only mammals that can fly. Some mammals, such as colugos and sugar gliders, use a flap of skin to glide from tree to tree, but only bats can flap their wings.

Most bats are nocturnal, so people see them less than other mammals. In all, about one thousand species of bats are found all over the world except for the polar regions. Chiroptera is divided into two suborders: Megachiroptera (large bats) and Microchiroptera (small bats). Megachiroptera is made up of one large family of 166 species of fruit bats. Microchiroptera contains sixteen families of mainly insect-eating bats.

Adapted for flight

Bats are specially adapted for flight in a number of ways. *Chiroptera* means "hand wing," which relates to the bat's wings. The wings are formed from skin stretched between the fingers and the body. The forelimb of the bat is different from that of other mammals. Some of its finger bones are as long as the bone in its forearm. These elongated fingers support the wing, holding it out in flight. Also, bats have a small, lightweight body, which means they have less weight to carry when they fly. Bats hang upside down by their legs when they rest. Their legs are weak and their knees bend backward rather than forward, as in other mammals. The legs of many bats, especially the larger species, are so weak that they crawl, instead of walk, on land.

Echolocation

Bats have well-developed senses. Megachiroptera bats hunt using sight and smell. They have large eyes to gather as much light as possible. Microchiroptera bats do not rely on sight. Instead, they use a natural type of sonar called echolocation to navigate and find food in the dark. They emit clicks from their voice box through their nose or mouth. The bats can detect sound waves as they bounce off objects, such as prey, in the bats' path. Bats identify the size and shape of an object— down to as small as the thickness of a pencil line on paper— by the sound of the echo. Some bats have a peculiar-looking fleshy structure, called a nose leaf, surrounding their nose that helps produce and direct their chirps.

KEY CHARACTERISTICS
CHIROPTERA

- **The only mammals that fly.**
- **Four elongated fingers support the skin that forms each wing.**
- **Clawed "thumbs."**
- **Weak legs; backward-bending knees; most crawl instead of walk on land.**
- **Teeth adapted to diet.**
- **Excellent hearing; about half of the species use echolocation.**

In echolocation, the bat produces sounds that bounce off objects. The bat's ears detect the echoes.

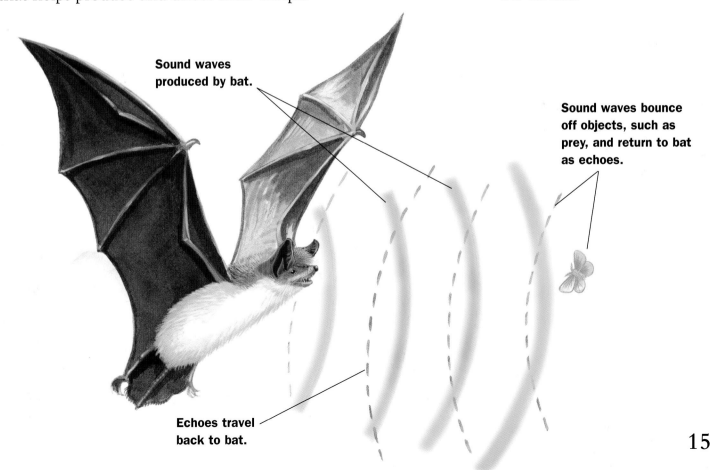

Sound waves produced by bat.

Sound waves bounce off objects, such as prey, and return to bat as echoes.

Echoes travel back to bat.

Pollination

Bats play an important role in the pollination of flowers and fruit trees. Fruit bats feed on fruits and the nectar of flowers using their extra-long tongue to reach deep into the flower. When they visit a flower to drink nectar, pollen sticks to their bodies, and they carry it to other flowers, pollinating them. Bats also help disperse the seeds of these plants. When the bats eat fruit, the seeds pass through their gut and out in their droppings (called guano).

Bat food

Microchiroptera bats eat a variety of foods, especially insects, that they catch in the air. Fisherman bats take fish from rivers, scooping up fish just under the surface with their long claws. Vampire bats feed on blood. This type of bat flies at dusk in search of a suitable animal, such as a bird, horse, cow, or even a human. It lands beside the animal and crawls over to it on its weak legs. The bat then removes any feathers or hair covering the skin before biting the flesh. The incisor teeth at the front of its mouth are thin and pointed and slip easily through skin without the victim noticing. The bat then sucks blood for about thirty minutes. The bat's saliva contains an anti-clotting substance.

A vampire bat (*Desmodus rotundus*) licks the blood that oozes from the bite on a chicken's foot.

An insect-eating noctule bat (*Nytalus noctula*) rests by hanging from its feet.

Roosting and hibernation

Since bats are nocturnal, they spend the day resting in a roost, often with many other bats. The roost may be a loft, hollow tree, or cave. These places are safe from predators and sheltered from the weather. Tent-building bats build their own roost by biting through the large leaves of a palm or banana tree so that they fold over, creating a "tent." As many as fifty or so bats may shelter under such a tent. Fruit bats often roost in caves. At dusk, they stream out of the cave in search of food. Some bats hibernate through cold winters or they would not find enough food to survive. Hibernating bats come out of hibernation when the weather gets warmer.

PRIMATES (PRIMATA)

Monkeys, lemurs, apes, and humans belong to the order Primata. Apes, such as chimpanzees and gorillas, are humans' closest living relatives. About one hundred eighty species of primates live in forests in the warmer parts of the world.

Primates have a well-developed brain and are more intelligent than other mammals. Their large, forward-facing eyes provide three-dimensional (3-D) vision and allows them to judge distances. Most mammals have nails instead of claws on their fingers and toes. Primates are divided into two suborders: Strepsirhini (lemurs, lorises, pottos, and bush babies) and the Haplorhini (the higher primates, including monkeys and apes).

Stepsirhini

These small primates, such as the lemur and the bush baby, have a doglike face. Animals in this suborder have

Lemurs, such as this Coquerel's dwarf lemur (*Mirza coquerel*), live only on the tropical island of Madagascar.

KEY CHARACTERISTICS
PRIMATES
- **Well-developed brain.**
- **Forward-facing eyes for 3-D vision.**
- **Hands and feet adapted for grasping.**
- **Most have flat nails rather than claws.**

large eyes with excellent night vision. They live in trees, with hands and feet adapted for gripping.

Monkeys

Monkeys can be divided into two large groups: New World and Old World monkeys. Nose shape distinguishes these two groups. New World monkeys, such as marmosets and howlers, live in South America. Their nostrils are wide open, far apart, and face outward. Many have a prehensile tail that acts as a fifth limb and can grip branches. The tail helps the monkey balance and grip while traveling through the trees. Old World monkeys, including baboons and macaques, live in Africa and Asia. Their nostrils are narrow, close together, and point downward. They do not have a prehensile tail. They have a thick "sitting pad" that cushions their rear.

Apes

Hominoidae, the taxonomic family that includes apes, also includes gibbons, chimpanzees, bonobos, gorillas, orangutans, and humans. These primates (especially humans) have the largest brains and so are more intelligent than other primates. Most apes have a broad chest and shoulders that allow a great deal of movement. Apes' arms are longer than their legs. Their face is flattened, and they have powerful jaws. Apes do not have a tail. They grasp objects with their hands. They have opposable thumbs—their thumbs stick out at an angle so they can grip and manipulate objects. Chimpanzees and gorillas also have an opposable big toe on each hind limb.

A gorilla's foot has a large gap between the big toe and the other toes. It easily grips food and objects with its hind limbs.

Mature male Western lowland gorillas (*Gorilla gorilla*) grow silver-gray hairs across their back. They often are called silverbacks.

19

The spider monkey (*Ateles geoffroyi*) uses its long, prehensile tail as a fifth limb to grip branches as it swings through trees.

Adaptation to habitat

Most primates are well-adapted to forest life. Small monkeys run along tree branches. Heavier primates hang from branches with their long limbs instead. For example, the spider monkeys of South America wrap their prehensile tail around branches to provide balance and grip as they swing from branch to branch. Gibbons have a style of movement called brachiation, which means they swing hand-to-hand through the forest. Although orangutans also have long limbs, they have a heavier body, so they climb through the trees.

Living in groups

Most primates are social animals that live in family groups, except for orangutans, some lemurs, and bush babies. A family group usually consists of one or two males, a number of females, and their young of varying ages. Primates give birth to one or two offspring at a time. They care for their young for a long period, teaching them the skills they will need as adults. Other members of the group help tend to and defend the youngsters. Some primates, such as chimpanzees and spider monkeys, live in large groups of up to two hundred individuals. These groups occasionally split into a number of smaller groups.

Defending a territory

Primates are territorial. They live in a particular area of a forest and defend its boundaries. Smaller primates, such as lemurs, mark the boundaries of their territory with their scent. Other species advertise their presence using sound. The booming call of howler monkeys and siamang gibbons travel many miles (kilometers) through the forest every morning.

Active at night

Most Haplorhini mammals, including some monkeys and humans, are diurnal and sleep at night. Chimpanzees, gorillas, and apes make a nest of branches and leaves to sleep in during the day. The nest is raised off the forest floor. Most Strepsirhini mammals, such as lemurs, lorises, and bush babies, are nocturnal. Their eyes are adapted to function in ambient light, such as moonlight and starlight. A special reflective cell layer, called the tapetum lucidum, lines their eyes, bouncing light around inside the eyes and back out through the pupils, giving them excellent night vision. The exceptionally large, dishlike eyes of the tarsiers capture as much natural light at night as possible.

BIGGEST AND SMALLEST

The largest primate, the male gorilla, stands 6.2 feet (1.9 m) tall and weighs as much as 441 pounds (200 kg). The smallest primate, the red mouse lemur, is only about 4 inches (10 cm) long. It has a tail 2 inches (5 cm) long and weighs 1 ounce (28 g). The pygmy marmoset, the smallest monkey, is so small that it fits inside a teacup.

Japanese snow monkeys (*Macaque japonensis*) groom each other to keep their fur clean and remove parasites—such as ticks and fleas.

ANTEATERS, SLOTHS, AND ARMADILLOS (XENARTHRA)

The three-toed sloth (*Bradypus* sp.) hangs upside down from a tree using its hooked claws. Its thick fur is often home to algae, mites, ticks, and beetles.

Anteaters, armadillos, and sloths are unusual mammals. Although these animals differ greatly in appearance from one another, they are grouped together in the Xenarthra order. An arrangement of extra bones in their lower backbone sets them apart.

Xenarthra features

The order Xenarthra contains twenty-nine species, most of which are found in Central and South America. The nine-banded armadillo also lives in North America. Extra bones in the spine of the animals in this order give added strength and support. This support is essential to anteaters and armadillos because they dig using their powerful forelimbs equipped with long claws. The sloth needs the extra support because it spends most of the day hanging by its claws in the trees.

Armor plating

Hard armor plating covers the bodies of members of the armadillo family. The plates actually are hardened skin that protects the head, back, sides, and limbs. Bands around the middle of the plating give the armadillos flexibility, and allow them to roll into a ball for protection. The number of bands varies between different species. The giant armadillo has an extra-large third claw on its front limbs that it uses to rip up soil to find food.

Diet

Members of the Xenarthra order have either small, unspecialized teeth or—in the case of the anteater—no teeth at all. Armadillos and anteaters are mostly insectivores, feeding on termites and other insects, small birds, and rodents. Sloths are herbivores. They eat leaves, shoots, twigs, and fruit. Sloths spend most of their time feeding. When their stomach is full, it makes up one-third of their total body weight. The plants they eat are low in nutritional content and the digestion of the leaves takes weeks, so sloths live very slow lives.

This Brazilian three-banded armadillo (*Tolypeutes tricinctus*) is curled up in a protective ball.

Extra orders: pangolins and aardvarks

Pangolins have a similar body shape to armadillos, but they are not closely related. They belong to the order Pholidota. They have a body covered with scales made from hardened hair. They do not have any teeth, but their tongue is long and sticky—ideal for collecting ants and termites. Aardvarks belong to the order Tubulidentata. They lack body armor but are powerful diggers, and can dig out burrows that measure more than 33 feet (10 m) long. Aardvarks have a piglike face with a long snout and large ears. Their teeth are adapted to crushing hard-backed insects for food.

23

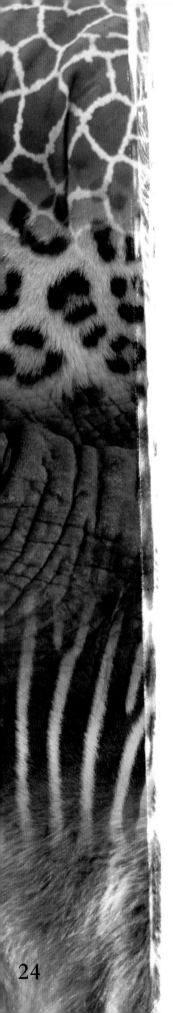

RODENTS (RODENTIA)

Rodents are gnawing animals, such as rats, mice, and squirrels. This order is the most varied and widespread of all mammals. Rodents can survive in almost all habitats, from deserts and grasslands to forests and marshes. They also live in the Arctic. In fact, there are more than two thousand different types of rodents— 40 percent of all mammals.

Squirrels, such as this red squirrel (*Scuirus vulgaris*), have a cylindrical-shaped body and a bushy tail, which is used for balance. They handle food with their front paws.

KEY CHARACTERISTICS
RODENTIA

- **Four incisors that grow continuously.**
- **No canine teeth, but a space called the diastema.**
- **Most walk on the soles of their feet.**
- **Keen senses of smell and hearing.**
- **Have whiskers.**

Rodent features

The order Rodentia is divided into three main groups: squirrel-like rodents, mouselike rodents, and cavy-like rodents. The main feature of rodents is their incredible gnawing ability, which results from a combination of their incisor teeth and powerful jaws. Four sharp, chisel-like incisors at the front of their mouth help them gnaw through almost anything. These teeth wear down but are replaced by new growth. In fact, the incisors never stop growing because the root of the tooth remains open, rather than closed as in other mammals. Rodents do not have canine teeth. Molars at the back of their mouth grind their food. Extra-large jaw muscles give them a powerful bite. Other features include a long tail, short legs with clawed toes, well-developed senses, and long whiskers.

Reproduction

Most rodents reproduce quickly. With the exception of the larger capybara and mara, rodents produce several offspring per litter. Some species of vole can produce thirteen litters in a single year. Many are ready to breed by the time they are two months old, so their reproductive rate is very high.

Pests

Many rodent species, particularly rats and mice, are considered pests. These rodents live close to people and are linked with disease. For example, in the fourteenth century, fleas that lived on rats helped spread bubonic plague throughout Europe, and millions of people died. Even now, rats and mice contaminate millions of tons (tonnes) of human food with their urine and feces. Rodents are becoming increasingly more resistant to the poisons traditionally used to control them.

Rodents, such as this brown rat (R*attus norvegicus*), give birth to hairless pink babies that must be cared for in a nest.

Rodents adapt quickly to new environments. Rats, for example, have hitchhiked all over the world with human explorers. Today, rats are found everywhere except in the polar regions. Rats are so successful because they are opportunists. They feed on a wide range of plant foods, such as seeds, fruits, and vegetables, as well as on the food waste of humans. Their excellent sense of smell helps them detect food stored inside buildings. Rats also are incredibly agile and can climb ropes and walls to gain entry to buildings and ships.

Building homes

Some rodents build elaborate homes. Squirrels build large dreys in trees using leaves and branches. Prairie dogs excavate an underground network of tunnels, known as a town, on grassland. They use the tunnels to escape predators and to raise their young. Some rodents actually have transformed the landscapes in which they live. Beavers, for example, use their teeth to fell branches and small trees to construct a dam across a river. This can create a lake that floods a valley. Once the new lake is at least 5 feet (1.5 m) deep, beavers build their home, called a lodge, along the shore or in the middle of the lake.

Surviving the cold

Rodents have a number of different ways of surviving cold weather. Mountain rodents, such as the chinchilla, which lives in the Andes, have thick fur to protect them from the cold. Other rodents, such as woodchucks, dormice, and marmots, survive winter by hibernating. They find a safe, dry nest site in which to spend the coldest months.

The ship rat, or black rat (*Rattus rattus*), can climb ropes. Rats often board ships at seaports and are carried around the world.

Extra order: lagomorphs

Rabbits may look like rodents, with their long, sharp incisors, but they are classified in a separate order called Lagomorpha. The word *Lagomorpha* means "hare-shaped." Forty-four species make up this order, which includes rabbits, hares, and pikas. Like rodents, the incisors of lagomorphs grow continuously, but they also have a second pair of small incisors, known as peg incisors. Rabbits and hares have large ears and long back legs that help them detect and run away from danger. As the prey of many predators, lagomorphs are well adapted for quick movement. Some hares can run at speeds of up to 5 miles (8 kilometers) per hour. Pikas are smaller than rabbits and hares. They look somewhat like guinea pigs, with rounded ears and short legs. Pikas live high in the mountains or underground in deserts in North America, eastern Europe, the Himalayas, and northern Asia.

CAPYBARAS

Capybaras of South America are the largest rodents in the world. They weigh as much as 141 pounds (64 kg). Capybaras behave like hippos. They spend the day wallowing in water and feeding on water plants, emerging at night to feed on grass and crops. When a predator approaches, the capybaras produce an alarm call and rush into the water, where they form a tight group. The young are safe in the center, while the adults stand around them, facing out.

The long ears of this black-tailed jack rabbit (*Lepus californicus*) give it excellent hearing to detect approaching predators.

WHALES, DOLPHINS, AND PORPOISES (CETACEA)

Whales, dolphins, and porpoises belong to the order Cetacea and are called cetaceans. Fossil evidence indicates that cetaceans evolved from land mammals millions of years ago. They are the only mammals, other than manatees and dugongs (*see page 31*), that are born, live, and die without ever leaving the water.

The female humpback whale (*Megaptera novaeangliea*) gives birth to a single calf underwater. She pushes it to the surface to take its first breath.

Cetacean features

Cetaceans breathe air through one or two blowholes on the top of their head that leads to the lungs. Their sleek, streamlined bodies slip through the water with ease. They have almost no hair—it would slow them down. They lack hind limbs, and their forelimbs are modified to form flippers. Cetaceans swim by moving their muscular tail up and down. They are easily distinguished from sharks and fish because their tail fluke lies horizontal to—instead of vertical to—the water's surface. Killer whales and shortfin pilot whales are the fastest cetaceans, swimming at speeds of up to 30 mph (48 kph).

Two groups

The more than seventy-seven species of cetaceans are divided into two groups: baleen whales and toothed whales. Baleen whales include the blue, fin, humpback, right, and sei whales. Instead of teeth, these whales filter small fish from the water using baleen plates in their mouth. Baleen is made of fingernail-like material that hangs down from the roof of their mouth. Toothed whales include dolphins, killer, and sperm whales. Their teeth are cone-shaped and point back into the mouth. This adaptation keeps fish from getting away.

Social behavior

Cetaceans develop strong relationships. The strongest tie occurs between mother and calf. The adults care for their young for at least a year. Many cetaceans travel in groups called pods. The toothed whales often hunt their prey in pods, migrate together, and even share the care of their young.

Whales and dolphins are acrobatic, and many jump out of the water in a movement called breaching. They slap the water as they come down. Biologists are unsure why whales breach—it may be to knock off skin parasites, for communication, or simply for fun. "Spy-hopping" is another cetacean activity that attests to the intelligence of these mammals: They sometimes poke their head out of the water to take a look around. Lobtailing is when whales stick their tail out of the water and then slap it on the water's surface to make a loud sound. This may serve as a warning to other whales in the group.

Dolphins, such as these common dolphins (*Delphinus delphis*), often travel together in large groups and may work together to capture shoals of fish.

Migration

Many cetaceans, especially baleen whales, migrate over long distances each year. They travel, sometimes in pods, from cold-water feeding grounds to warm-water breeding grounds. For example, gray whales spend the summer months in the Arctic Ocean and Bering Sea. The swim down the warmer Pacific coast of North America to Southern California and Mexico, where they spend the winter.

Finding food

Baleen whales are filter feeders. They feed on plankton, krill, and small fish. They gulp huge mouthfuls of water into their mouth and then push it out through their baleen plates, sieving (straining out) the food.

Toothed whales are predators that hunt their food. They chase prey such as squid, octopus, and fish. Killer whales hunt seals, penguins, and other whales, too. Dolphins and killer whales often work together to herd their prey in order to trap them. The sperm whale hunts for squid and giant octopus that live in deep water. Most dives are between 1,000 to 2,000 feet (300 to 600 m), but sperm whales may be able to dive as deep as 10,000 feet (3,048 m). They can stay underwater for up to two hours in order to reach such depths.

Toothed whales find their prey using sonar, or echolocation, just like bats. They emit

A blue whale (*Balaenoptera musculus*) and her calf swim along the coast of California during their annual migration.

high-frequency clicks that bounce off objects in their path. They also use the echoes to navigate in murky water.

Communicating

Whales communicate with each other using sound. Baleen whales sing low-frequency songs to attract mates and to help them keep track of members of the pod. By far, the song of the humpback whale, which lasts up to thirty minutes and can be heard over great distances, is the most famous. Beluga whales also sing to keep in contact. They are nicknamed "sea canaries." They produce a range of sounds including moos, chirps, and whistles. Some of these sounds are audible through the air. Sperm whales produce clicks. Individual sperm whales each produce a particular pattern of clicks called "codas" that are repeated at intervals.

Extra order: Sirenia

Dugongs and manatees may resemble whales somewhat, but they are placed in the order Sirenia. There are three species of manatee and one species of dugong. All are large, slow-moving mammals that feed solely on plants. They have paddlelike front limbs and a flat, broad tail that they use to propel themselves through the water.

BIGGEST AND SMALLEST

The blue whale (*Balaenoptera musculus*) is the largest animal that has ever lived. It grows to about 95 feet (29 m) long and weighs as much as twenty-five bull elephants. These enormous animals eat about 4.4 tons (4 tonnes) of krill daily. Adult blue whales have no predators except humans. The smallest whale is the dwarf sperm whale (*Kogia simus*), which measures only 8.5 feet (2.6 m) long.

Manatees, such as this West Indian manatee (*Trechechus manatus*), prefer shallow water with plenty of their favorite food—sea grass.

31

CARNIVORES (CARNIVORA)

Lions, wolves, foxes, and bears are all members of the order Carnivora. The word *carnivore* is often defined as "an animal that eats meat." Many carnivores in this order, however, do not eat just meat. These mammals are grouped together because of features of their anatomy that are linked to their diet.

There are approximately 230 species in the order Carnivora. This order includes smaller members, such as weasels and stoats, civets, and mongooses, as well as larger ones, such as brown bears and tigers. There are some amphibious species, too. Seals and walruses live in the sea and come onto land to give birth to their pups. Otters usually hunt in water, but spend the rest of their time on land. Some otters live in freshwater rivers, while sea otters live in coastal waters, such as those along the Pacific coast of North America.

Herbivorous giant pandas (*Ailuropoda melanoleuca*) feed mostly on bamboo shoots. An enlarged wrist bone that sticks out helps the pandas grip bamboo stems.

Teeth and claws

The main feature of carnivores is their specialized teeth adapted to a diet of eating mostly meat. Their teeth must grip and tear the flesh of their prey. They have small incisors at the front of the mouth for gripping and nibbling meat off bones and for grooming their fur. Four long, curved canines stab and grab prey. Large premolars and molars with jagged edges behind the canines slice through flesh. The carnassials—the fourth upper premolar and the first lower molar—are larger than the others. Carnivores also have powerful jaw muscles essential for holding onto and biting into prey animals. They swallow chunks of food without chewing, so their stomachs are adapted to digesting large pieces of meat.

Carnivores have four or five long, curved claws on each foot. Cats can retract (withdraw) their claws while sneaking up silently on prey. Cats then use their claws to lock onto and pull down prey.

Well-developed senses

Most carnivores are predators with well-developed senses for locating prey. They have excellent eyesight and hearing and a good sense of smell. Whiskers around the nose of some carnivores increase their tactile (touching) sensations. Forward-facing eyes provide 3-D vision, essential for judging distances. Many carnivores are better at detecting movement than seeing detail. Carnivores may not spot a well-camouflaged prey animal unless it moves.

KEY CHARACTERISTICS
CARNIVORA

- **Four large canine teeth for stabbing and gripping prey.**
- **Four carnassial teeth for shearing through meat and bone.**
- **Well-developed senses, especially sight and hearing.**
- **Four or five toes with sharp claws.**

The large canines of this lion (*Panthera leo*) are easily visible when it opens its mouth.

Hunting together

A carnivore's survival depends on whether it can catch enough food. Older or sick individuals often starve to death because they are unable to catch prey. They may be forced to scavenge for food or attack easy prey, such as people. Some carnivores, such as lions and wolves, sometimes work together to catch food while others, such as tigers and foxes, prefer to hunt alone.

Lions live in groups called prides on the open savannas of southern and eastern Africa. A pride consists of an adult male, several lionesses, and their cubs. The lionesses work together to catch prey. One lioness approaches the prey animals, forcing them to move toward the other lionesses who are lying in wait. Lions must get closer to their prey than other predators, such as the cheetah, because they cannot run as far or as fast. Several lionesses hunting together can bring down large prey, such as wildebeest and cape buffalo.

Lionesses (*Panthera leo*) creep to within 98 feet (30 m) of their prey before they charge, pulling it down with their claws before giving a deadly bite to the throat. They are attacking a young cape buffalo (*Syncerus caffer*).

SEALS AND SEA LIONS

Walruses, seals, and sea lions are adapted to living in water, but females give birth on land. True seals have no external ears, and their back flippers point backward. Sea lions and fur seals have small external ears and back flippers that can twist forward for moving on land. Walruses have a distinctive pair of tusks. Only walruses and eared seals can support themselves on their front flippers on land.

Feeding on salmon

The grizzly, or brown, bear is the largest land carnivore. It feeds on a wide-ranging diet that includes insects and small mammals as well as roots and fungi. In autumn, the brown bear must eat fatty food to build up enough body fat for its hibernation. Many brown bears live along rivers in the autumn, feeding on salmon that are migrating upstream to breed. Salmon is rich in protein and fat, and the bears put on a lot of weight by eating this fish.

Surviving the cold

Some carnivores, including the polar bear, Arctic fox, walrus, and some of the seals and sea lions, survive the extreme cold of the polar regions. The Weddell seal, for example, can tolerate an air temperature of -40 °F (-40 °C) while lying on the ice. The bodies of these polar mammals are specially adapted so that they retain as much of their body heat as possible. As well as thick fur, they have a layer of blubber (fat) beneath the skin. Polar bears also have black skin that absorbs heat from sunlight. Their white, hollow hairs not only help insulate them, but also conduct the sunlight to their skin.

Brown, or grizzly, bears (*Ursus arctos*) feast on salmon in the autumn to build up body fat before hibernation.

ELEPHANTS (PROBOSCIDEA)

These young African bull elephants (*Loxodonta africana*) are carrying out a mock fight.

The African elephant is the largest land animal. Only three species of elephants currently exist, but in prehistoric times there may have been more than three hundred different species. Elephants are long-lived mammals, with some individuals reaching seventy to eighty years of age.

Giant plant eaters

Elephants belong to the order Proboscidea. The three species are the African, African forest, and Asian elephants. All are herbivorous. The African elephant lives on the African savanna. The African forest elephant is found in the dense forests of eastern Africa, while the Asian elephant is widespread across India and Southeast Asia—in mostly forest habitats.

Trunks, tusks, and ears

One of the most noticeable features of the elephant is its trunk. The trunk is long and muscular, and formed from the upper lip and nose. Elephants use their trunk like a fifth limb for touching, handling food, and drinking water. Their huge teeth are flat with ridges, ideal for grinding plant material. Elephants have six sets of teeth during their lifetime, with each set consisting of four huge teeth. There are two teeth in the upper jaw and two in the lower jaw. Elephant tusks are elongated upper incisor teeth. They first appear when the elephant is two years old and continue to grow throughout its life. All elephants have tusks, but the tusks of female Asian elephants are small and do not protrude beyond the lips. Elephant ears are large, too, especially those of the African elephant. They are well supplied with blood vessels. Elephants flap their ears to help stay cool.

Living in herds

Elephants live in herds, with the adult males and females living separately. Female elephants live together in family groups led by the oldest female, known as the matriarch. Bull elephants leave the family group and live either with other bulls or alone. They join the females only to breed. When a male elephant is ready to breed, "comes into musk" and acts aggressively toward other bulls.

Adapting to their environment

Some African elephants live in semiarid areas of southwest Africa. They have slightly longer legs that allow them to walk longer distances in search of water. Some elephants have learned to use their tusks to dig for salt in caves. The forest elephant looks very similar to the African elephant, although it is slightly shorter. It moves more easily through the dense forest.

Extra order: Hyracoidea (rock and bush hyraxes)

Although it looks nothing like an elephant, the hyrax is one of the closest living relatives to the elephant. The hyrax and elephant both have ridged teeth, similar foot bones, and flat toenails. Hyraxes' long incisor teeth grow continuously. They have a scent gland on their back.

KEY CHARACTERISTICS
PROBOSCIDEA

- Trunk formed from upper lip and nose.
- Tusks formed from upper incisors.
- Skeleton made of heavy bones to support the animal's great weight.
- Large, fan-shaped ears help keep animals cool.

The rock hyrax (*Procavia capensis*) is a small, brown mammal that lives in rocky outcrops where it feeds on plants.

UNGULATES (PERISSODACTYLA AND ARTIODACTYLA)

The black rhino (*Diceros bicornis*) has an odd number of toes. It uses its prehensile upper lip to browse on the twigs and new shoots of bushes and low trees.

Ungulates is the general name for a large group of mammals that have hooves. Hooves are modified toenails that help ungulates run fast.

Two orders

Ungulates are divided into two orders: Perissodactyla and Artiodactyla. Members of Perissodactyla have an odd number of toes, either one or three. This order contains seventeen species of horses, zebras, tapirs, and rhinos. Artiodactyls have an even number of toes, either two or four. There are more than two hundred species of even-toed artiodactyls, including pigs, camels, llamas, deer, giraffe, sheep, and goats.

Ungulate features

Ungulates have four long limbs, with bones arranged in a different way from other mammals. The bones in ungulates' feet are long and fused together. The foot is held in such a way that only the very tips of the toes touch the ground. Millions of years ago, each toe ended in a hoof. Over time, the feet evolved so that some of the toes fused together. Present-day ungulates have between one and four toes. The edge of the hoof is thickened with a tough material called keratin. It is strong enough to support the weight of the animal's body. Keratin is the same material that forms hair and nails.

Teeth and digestion

Ungulates have long jaws with teeth adapted to eating plants, especially grass. The teeth are large and ridged so they can grind food. Many artiodactyls are ruminants—animals with a stomach that has three or four chambers. The animals chew and swallow their food before regurgitating it into their mouth so they can chew it again. This helps break down their food and eases digestion. Ruminants also have microorganisms in their stomach that help digest the tough plant food.

Horns, antlers, and tusks

Many ungulates have bony outgrowths, such as horns and antlers, which they use as weapons. Antelope and cattle have permanent horns with bone in the middle. Deer antlers also are made from bone, but they are shed each year and replaced by a new set. As a deer gets older, the antlers get larger. Pigs and hippos have tusks— large teeth that grow from their jawbones and protrude on either side of their face. They use their tusks for fighting, defense, or digging up roots. The rhino's horn is different. It is made from compressed hairs instead of bone.

The red deer stag (*Cervus elaphus*) has an impressive set of branched antlers that are shed and regrown each year. During the breeding season, the stags fight, locking their antlers with their heads down. They push and twist each other until one gives up.

Herds

Many ungulates, such as antelope and zebras, live in herds. This provides greater safety, especially for young animals in the herd. The young can run within minutes of being born—an ability essential to survival for these prey animals.

The African savanna is home to many different types of ungulates, all living close together. They feed on different foods, so they do not compete with each other. Some graze on grass, while others browse on low shrubs or tall trees. The smaller antelopes, for example, feed on the lower branches of trees and on shrubs, while giraffes can reach the higher branches.

Migrating

Many ungulates migrate in search of food. Huge herds of wildebeest and zebras move north from the Serengeti Plain in Tanzania to find fresh grazing in Kenya. They cross wide rivers along the way, and some of the herd drown or are killed by crocodiles in the water. Later in the year, the herds return to the Serengeti. In North America, herds of caribou migrate north to find summer grazing in the Arctic, and then migrate back to the shelter of the forests for the winter.

Its long tongue, neck, and legs allow the giraffe (*Giraffa camelopardalis*) to feed on the upper branches of acacia trees. A giraffe's tongue can measure up to 18 inches (46 cm) long.

Desert survival

The camel is adapted to life in the desert. It has a hump containing fat stores, and it can survive for weeks without water because of its amazing metabolism. Its body temperature rises by a few degrees during the day, which reduces the amount of water the camel loses because it does not need to sweat. In extremely hot conditions, the camel sits with its rear end facing the Sun. Only a small surface is exposed to the Sun, so it absorbs less heat. Deserts can become cold at night, and the camel loses excess heat. By morning, its body temperature has fallen back to normal.

Arctic cold

Reindeer live on the bleak Arctic plains and in the surrounding forests. They have adapted to their freezing winter climate. They live in herds that range in size from about twenty animals to several thousand. The herds constantly are on the move looking for food. They eat lichens, tough grasses, and the leaves of low-growing trees. In winter, they dig through the snow in search of lichen and moss.

Huge herds of wildebeest (*Connochaetes taurinus*) must cross rivers when migrating. During the river crossing, many wildebeest are attacked by crocodiles. Calves sometimes wash away in the strong river currents.

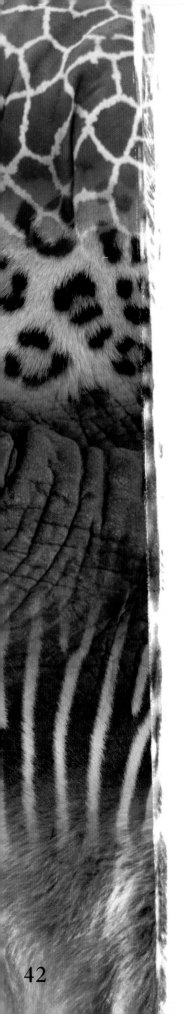

UNDER THREAT

Many species of mammals are under threat around the world. Familiar animals, such as the tiger, snow leopard, giant panda, and rhino, could become extinct in the wild within the next thirty years.

Loss of habitat

The main reason for the decline in mammal numbers is loss of habitat. As the human population increases, more land is needed and more habitats are lost. Habitats, such as forest, grassland, and even desert, are being cleared to make more space for houses, factories, and roads. Grassland is plowed up and replaced by farmland. Trees are felled for timber and fuelwood. Some of the world's most important habitats are the tropical and temperate rain forests—home to more species of animals and plants than any other habitats. Sadly, these valuable forests are being cleared at an ever-increasing rate. Habitats for tigers, jaguars, Asian elephants, gorillas, orangutans, and other mammals are disappearing quickly.

This shop sells tiger skins and a variety of "medicinal" products, many of which come from endangered animals.

Pollution also damages habitats. Air pollution from cars and factories creates acid rain that kills trees. Raw sewage, chemicals, and oil spills pollute waterways, harming marine mammals, such as dolphins, seals, and sea otters.

Hunting

Many mammals are hunted for their fur, tusks, or horns. Snow leopards and other cats, bears, and foxes are shot to make fur coats. Elephants are killed for their ivory tusks; rhinos for their horns. International laws have attempted to stop the trade in ivory and in many furs, but much killing continues illegally. Tigers are killed because some people believe that their bones and organs have medicinal or religious value.

Success stories

Some mammals have been saved from extinction. The gray whale was removed from the endangered species list because its numbers have increased. The golden lion tamarin from the South American rain forest was bred successfully in zoos and some were released back into the rain forest. The Przewalski's horses once roamed the plains of central Asia, but the species became extinct in the wild. Fortunately, some survived in zoos, where they have bred successfully. Plans are in place to reintroduce the horses to their native habitats. Such captive-breeding practices work only if the animals' habitats are protected. Once their habitats disappear, the animals can never be reintroduced into the wild.

In 1980, there were fewer than one hundred golden lion tamarins (*Leontopithecus rosalia rosalia*) left in the world. Thanks to captive breeding, that total has increased to more than one thousand.

43

MAMMAL CLASSIFICATION

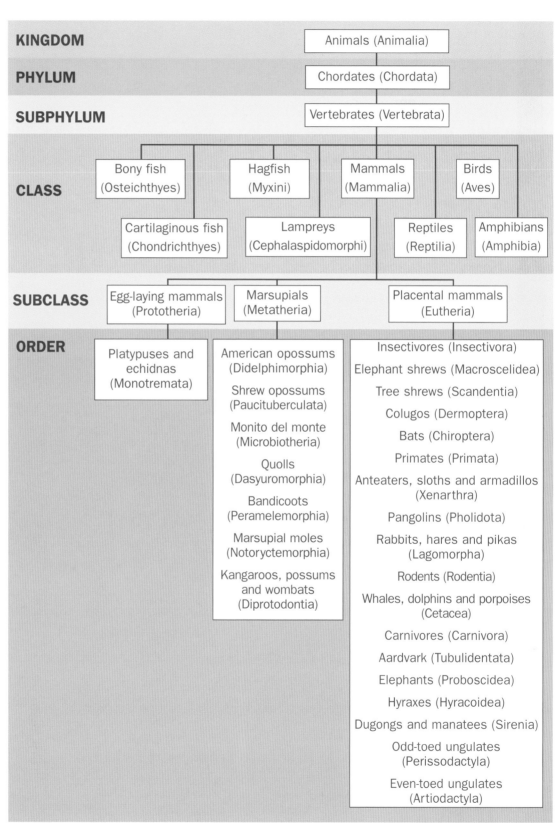

KINGDOM	Animals (Animalia)
PHYLUM	Chordates (Chordata)
SUBPHYLUM	Vertebrates (Vertebrata)

CLASS

Bony fish (Osteichthyes)

Cartilaginous fish (Chondrichthyes)

Hagfish (Myxini)

Lampreys (Cephalaspidomorphi)

Mammals (Mammalia)

Reptiles (Reptilia)

Birds (Aves)

Amphibians (Amphibia)

SUBCLASS

Egg-laying mammals (Prototheria)

Marsupials (Metatheria)

Placental mammals (Eutheria)

ORDER

Platypuses and echidnas (Monotremata)

American opossums (Didelphimorphia)

Shrew opossums (Paucituberculata)

Monito del monte (Microbiotheria)

Quolls (Dasyuromorphia)

Bandicoots (Peramelemorphia)

Marsupial moles (Notoryctemorphia)

Kangaroos, possums and wombats (Diprotodontia)

Insectivores (Insectivora)

Elephant shrews (Macroscelidea)

Tree shrews (Scandentia)

Colugos (Dermoptera)

Bats (Chiroptera)

Primates (Primata)

Anteaters, sloths and armadillos (Xenarthra)

Pangolins (Pholidota)

Rabbits, hares and pikas (Lagomorpha)

Rodents (Rodentia)

Whales, dolphins and porpoises (Cetacea)

Carnivores (Carnivora)

Aardvark (Tubulidentata)

Elephants (Proboscidea)

Hyraxes (Hyracoidea)

Dugongs and manatees (Sirenia)

Odd-toed ungulates (Perissodactyla)

Even-toed ungulates (Artiodactyla)

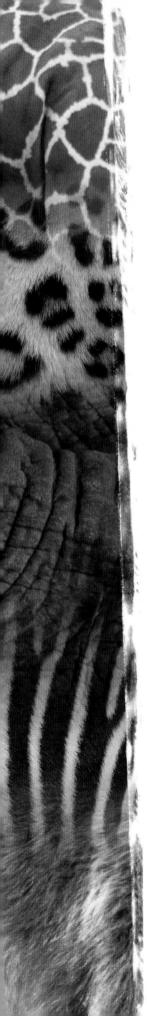

GLOSSARY

adapt to change to fit with the surrounding environment.

amphibious an animal that is adapted to living on both land and in water at certain times of its life.

anatomy parts of the body.

aquatic living in water.

baleen plates fibrous mouth plates in some whale species that filter food from the water.

blubber a thick layer of fat just beneath the skin of marine mammals, such as whales and seals, that traps heat in the body.

brachiation the term for a gibbon's movements as it swings through trees using only its arms.

breaching jumping straight up and out of the water by cetaceans.

bubonic plague a disease that causes fever and painful swelling of the lymph glands; spread by fleas on rats.

canine tooth a long, prominent tooth near the front of the mouth between the incisors and premolars. Most mammals have four canine teeth.

carnivore an animal that hunts and eats other animals; also, a member of the order Carnivora.

clot to congeal or stick together.

digest to break down food into simple substances the body can use.

diurnal active in the daytime.

drey a squirrel's nest.

echolocation a method for locating objects using sound.

endangered at risk of a severe drop in population or of becoming extinct.

endothermic warm-blooded; able to produce and maintain a stable body temperature, regardless of the temperature of the surroundings.

evolved changed over generations.

extinct no longer in existence and having no chance of ever again existing in its original form.

filter to sieve, sift, or strain small particles from a liquid.

flipper the modified forearm of a seal or whale that helps it swim.

guano bat and bird droppings.

habitat the natural environment of a plant or animal.

herbivore an animal that eats only plant foods.

hibernation a long, deep winter sleep during which an animal's metabolism slows down.

incisors the small teeth found at the front of the mouth.

ivory the creamy, yellow/white, hard covering of the tusks of elephants and walruses; also the tusks themselves.

krill shoals of small crustaceans found in the upper layer of the oceans; the main food of baleen whales.

lichen an organism consisting of an alga and fungus living together.

mammal a warm-blooded, hair-covered animal with mammary glands that in the female produce milk for the young.

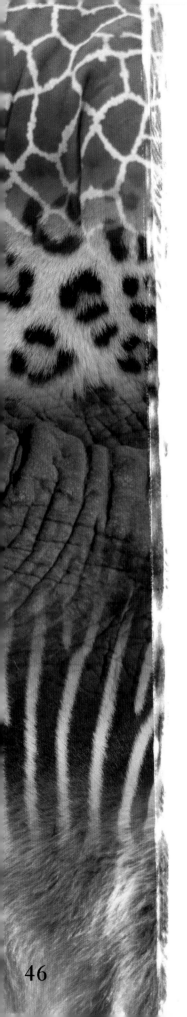

GLOSSARY (CONTINUED)

marsupial a mammal whose young develop in a pouch after birth.

matriarch the female leader of an animal family, such as the matriarch of a herd of elephants.

metabolism chemical reactions that occur inside living organisms to provide energy and maintain the body.

migrate to make seasonal journeys between locations.

molar a large tooth at the back of the mouth used for chewing and grinding.

monotreme an egg-laying mammal, such as the platypus and echidna.

nectar the sugary fluid produced by flowers.

nocturnal active at night.

omnivore an animal that eats a diet of both plant and animal foods.

opportunist an animal that deals with changes by taking advantage of situations to best benefit itself.

opposable thumb/toe a thumb or big toe that sticks out at an angle to the fingers or toes and allows the animal to grip and manipulate objects.

parasite an organism that lives on or in another organism and causes the host organism harm.

pest an animal present in large numbers that damage crops, spread diseases, or annoy other animals.

placental mammal a mammal that gets it nourishment during development from a placenta while inside its mother's body.

plankton tiny plant and animal organisms that float in water.

pod a group of whales.

predator an animal that hunts and eats other animals.

prehensile having the ability to wrap around objects; for example, the trunk of an elephant, the tongue of a giraffe, or the tail of a monkey.

prey an animal that is hunted by a predator for food.

rabies a deadly viral disease that affects the central nervous system.

regurgitate to bring up undigested food from the stomach into the mouth to chew again or to expel from the body to feed young.

reintroduce to release an animal back into its native habitat.

ruminant a mammal with a specialized stomach adapted to digesting grass and other plant foods.

savanna a grassland habitat with a few trees found in tropical parts of Africa.

scavenge to feed on the bodies of dead animals or rotting plant matter.

species a unique, specific organism that differs from all others.

streamlined a smooth shape that slips easily through air and water.

tail fluke the powerful, double-lobed, horizontally oriented tip of a whale's tail that propels it through the water.

tapetum lucidum a reflective layer that lines the eyes of certain mammals and helps capture all available light. It also makes animals' eyes "glow."

vertebrate an animal with a backbone.

FURTHER INFORMATION

BOOKS

Attenborough, David. *Life of Mammals*. BBC Books (2002).

Cahill, Tim. *Dolphins*. National Geographic (2003).

DK Animal Encyclopedia. Dorling Kindersley (2000).

Forshaw, Gould, and McKay, eds. *The Encyclopedia of Animals: Mammals, Birds, Reptiles, Amphibians*. Fog City Press (2002).

Ganeri, Anita. *Animal Groupings*. *Nature Files* (series). Chelsea House (2004).

Hogan, Linda and Brenda Peterson. *Sightings: The Gray Whale's Mysterious Journey*. National Geographic (2003).

Macdonald, David, ed. *The New Encyclopedia of Mammals*. Oxford University Press (2001).

McKay, George, et al. *The Encyclopedia of Animals: A Complete Visual Guide*. University of California Press (2004).

Morgan, Sally. *Animal Kingdom: Mammals*. Raintree (2004).

Solway, Andrew. *Classifying Living Things: Classifying Mammals*. Heinemann Library (2003).

Spilsbury, Richard. *Classification: From Mammals to Fungi*. *Science Answers* (series). Heinemann Library (2004).

Taylor, Barbara. *Visual Encyclopedia of Animals*. Dorling Kindersley (2000).

Wallace, Holly. *Classification*. *Life Processes* (series). Heinemann Library (2002).

WEB SITES

http://animaldiversity.ummz.umich.edu/site/accounts/information/Mammalia.html
Explore the mammals link of the University of Michigan's Animal Diversity Web site.

http://members.aol.com/bats4kids/
Discover everything you want to know about bats.

http://whozoo.org/mammals/mammals.htm
Visit the mammals at the Fort Worth Zoo in Texas and follow the links to cool facts.

www.nationalgeographic.com/kids/bookworm/mammal.html
Take a short mammal quiz and then explore National Geographic's Web site for more information on mammals.

www.savethetigerfund.org/Directory/kids.htm
Learn all you can about the five remaining tiger species and their conservation.

www.ucmp.berkeley.edu/mammal/mammal.html
Join a quagga, an extinct mammal, on a quest for more knowledge about mammals.

INDEX

Page numbers in **bold** refer to a photograph or illustration.